Let's Take Care of Our New Turtle

Alejandro Algarra
Rosa M. Curto

A very special surprise

John and his little sister, Sally, are going to have a very big surprise soon. Since a few days ago, Mom and Dad have been preparing a large aquarium with several gadgets, but they haven't told the children what animal they're going to put in there yet. Mom has only given them one clue: It's an animal with a shell. Sally tries to guess what it might be: a snail? Maybe it's a turtle?

The surprise pet is...

A turtle! Sally and John are very happy. As soon as they arrive home from the shop, Dad puts the turtle in a small aquarium that they had kept in the attic. "You can't touch him yet, kids. Wait a few days and I'll let you know when he settles in permanently." John asked, "Why don't you put him in the large aquarium that you've prepared?" Mom and Dad explained that the children would have to wait a few days, until they take the turtle to the veterinarian and analyze his "little poos."

A very original name

Everything went all right at the vet's and the turtle, which was very healthy, is in his permanent house. John and Sally thought of a name that they both liked for their pet. It took them a long time to decide, but in the end, they agreed that the turtle would be called Shelly. It's a very original name! When Mom came home, everything was already prepared to place him in his permanent home. Sally and John cried out loudly: "The turtle is called Shelly!"

Green body and red ears

What's John and Sally's turtle like? He's a red-eared slider. On both sides of his head, just behind the ears, he has a bright red marking. But they're not ears! Turtles, like all other reptiles like snakes and lizards, don't have ears. They're aquatic and they like living in a warm environment and sunbathing for most of the day. Furthermore, they are very good swimmers. When they bought the turtle, he measured about 4 inches (10 cm). Shops aren't allowed to sell smaller turtles, to guarantee that they are strong and healthy when they arrive home.

What is Shelly's house like?

Shelly has found himself in a very cozy aquarium/terrarium:

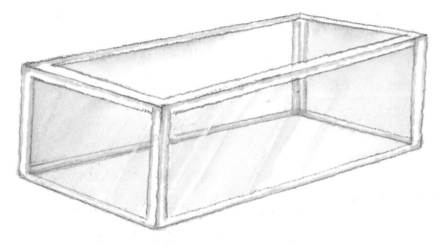

Aquarium/terrarium: It must be large enough for the turtle to swim freely when it grows up.

Equipment: A water filter must be installed to keep the water clean with a heater for aquariums, to maintain the water at an adequate temperature.

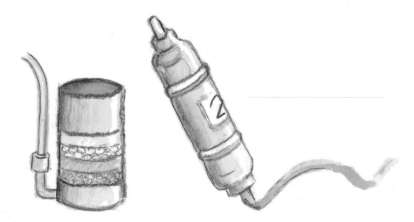

Lighting: The turtle needs an ultraviolet light, which will help it to grow big and strong, and a normal light (can be a fluorescent one), which must be turned on for eight to twelve hours per day.

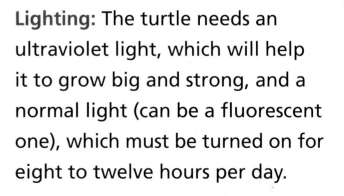

Sand: The bottom of the aquarium should be covered with a layer of sand.

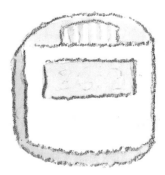

Thermometers: One monitors the water temperature and the other that of the dry area.

Dry area: This platform allows the turtle to rest on firm ground, bathe in the heat and light, and you can give him some of his food here during the first few days.

It can be built in several ways.

Feeding aquarium: In order to keep the main aquarium clean longer, it's better to feed the turtle in a separate small aquarium (with water and a dry area).

The first bath

The first time that Shelly entered his aquarium, he hid inside his shell. He's a bit scared, because he's just spent a few quite busy days. Little by little, he takes out his little legs and pokes his head out to see what his house is like and if

everything's peaceful. Finally, Shelly decides to dive into the water for the first time. "Look, John! Look at him swimming!" When he gets to the bottom, the turtle hides underneath a roof tile that Mom had put there. "Good, but, of course, he'll have to come up to breathe later!"

Cleaning the aquarium

Shelly's aquarium water must be kept very clean so that he doesn't get sick. If it isn't cleaned often, it will get full of his "little poos" and food leftovers and will end up smelling really bad. Every two or three days, the children help Mom and Dad to change part of the water. And about every two or three weeks, it must be cleaned completely: All the water is changed; the dry area is cleaned thoroughly, including the stones and crystals in the aquarium. Shelly is going to be very healthy if the children always keep his house clean!

It's dinner time

Shelly likes to eat a little bit of everything. He has a very varied diet, including fruits and vegetables, a little meat, and special turtle food. Today, it's Sally's turn to feed him. First she places some clean fresh lettuce leaves in the dry area. Then she scatters a pinch of turtle food pellets into the water.

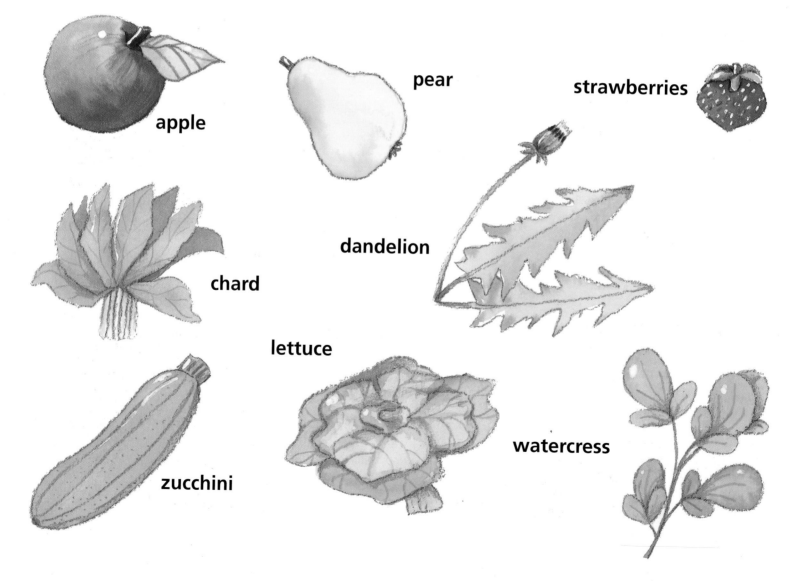

apple

pear

strawberries

chard

dandelion

lettuce

zucchini

watercress

To finish, she adds some meat cubes, which Shelly loves. Mom has taken advantage of the fact that they're feeding him meat today, to mix it with some calcium powder. Then the turtle's shell and bones will grow healthy and strong. Be careful! You should never give a turtle more than he can eat in about fifteen minutes, and only give him meat as a treat, not all the time.

prepared food

calcium

nutrients

vitamins

cooked, diced chicken

food sticks

fresh food for cats and dogs

diced meat

Heat bathing

There's nothing that Shelly likes better than lying underneath the lamp that serves as a heater. Reptiles are cold-blooded animals and they need to warm themselves up before doing any activity. The turtle lies under the light and stretches out his neck and legs. Sally asked: "Why don't we move the lamp closer to him?" "Because he might get burned! He must never be able to touch the lamp," replied John. "Furthermore," said Dad, "it's important for the lamp to be well connected and supported, to avoid any kind of accident with the water."

A special fluorescent lamp

Sally has realized that one of the two fluorescent lamps on the aquarium lid is purple. Why is it like that? How strange! ... John explained to her what it's for: It's an ultraviolet light. The turtle needs it to keep his shell nice and hard and to have strong bones. Just like people, turtles need ultraviolet light to make a very important vitamin: vitamin D. We also take ultraviolet light from the sun, but since the turtle lives in the aquarium, we give him this special light. Without it, Shelly would be sad, he'd eat less, and he could get a shell illness. "Phew! It's lucky we put it there!" said Sally.

Very clean hands

Shelly has already spent a few weeks in the aquarium and is gradually getting used to it. John is curious to touch the turtle and find out what Shelly feels like. "I want to touch him too," said Sally. She can't hold him yet: Her hands are too small and he might fall. Before picking up a turtle and especially afterward, you must wash your hands thoroughly. John picked up Shelly with both hands, grasping him by the shell. It's good if Shelly is able to put his claws on John's hands. Then he won't feel a void underneath his feet and he'll feel more secure.

Shelly's friends

"Dad, could we have another turtle in the aquarium to keep Shelly company?" asked John. "That's not a good idea." Dad explained to the children that red-eared sliders prefer to live alone. "If we had a larger aquarium, we could have another turtle. In our aquarium, there might not be enough space and they would fight. Don't worry about Shelly not having enough company here at home. We are his friends."

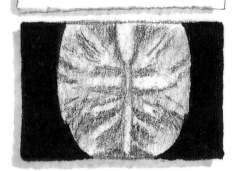 

Shelly is sick

Sally has noticed that Shelly is acting a bit funny lately. He spends a lot of time inside his shell and eats less. The other day, Sally saw him moving a bit strangely in the water, as if he were coughing. It looks like Shelly has got a bit of a cold. We must take him to the veterinarian. Reptiles have a special veterinarian, where pets like frogs, geckos, and turtles go. The veterinarian is going to give him an injection of antibiotics, and the family is going to move the aquarium to another place where there is less draft. Drafts are very bad for turtles! Luckily, it won't take Shelly very long to get well.

Don't do that!

John has found out that a friend in his class has let his turtle go in a pond near school. "Why did he do that?" asked Mom. "He told me the aquarium had gotten too small for him and they didn't want to buy a bigger one," replied John. "We would never do that with Shelly," said Mom angrily. When you buy a pet, it must be perfectly clear that you must look after it for as long as it lives. Many of the turtles that people set free in ponds and lakes die of cold or hunger. And many others survive and displace the other wild turtles that live there. You can take them to a zoo or a pet shop or find them a new owner, but you must never release them into the wild.

After so many years...

When the children have grown up and left home, Shelly will still be with the family. Red-eared sliders live for about twenty-five years; some reach over forty. John and Sally's children might even get to meet Shelly. It's a nice scenario: The grandchildren will visit their grandparents' house and spend the afternoon entertained watching old Shelly, who is still as happy as the first day, after so many years. The turtle looks at everyone from the aquarium, winks at them, and dives into the water to refresh himself. Good-bye Shelly!

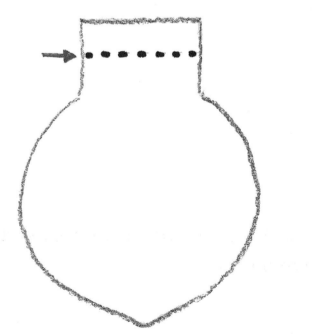

Turtle box

Materials: glue, green cardboard, white paper, green and yellow waterco
paints, paintbrush, cardboard egg carton, black felt pen, and scissors.

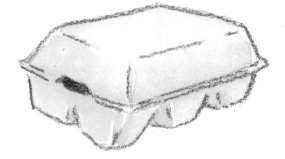

Instructions:

1. Paint the box in different shades of green and patches or yellow stripes and leave it to dry.
2. Trace the pattern of the head on the green cardboard and cut it out.
3. Draw a triangle for the tail on the green cardboard and cut it out.
4. Make the eyes on the white paper and cut them out. Glue them on the head. Draw the iris on the eyes and the nostrils with the black pen, as shown in the illustration. If you like, you can also draw eyelids.
5. When the box is dry, attach the turtle's head at the dotted line, as indicated by the arrow. Attach the tail to the other end.

Now you have an amusing turtle box for keeping little things like beads for making necklaces, marbles, and small treasures.

Advice from the veterinarian

A very long-living pet

The red-eared slider, also known as the Florida turtle, is one of the most popular turtles in the world. With simple care, good health supervision, and appropriate feeding, they can keep you company for a lifetime. Like all other pets, the turtle is not a toy, but rather a living creature with a series of special needs to be taken care of. To begin with, the typical small containers with small plastic palm trees, sold in many shops to house turtles, are inadvisable. Before purchasing, you should find out about what things you need and prepare them at home beforehand, and then choose the most appropriate specimen in the pet shop.

The size of the aquarium

In order for the turtle to be comfortable, you should provide it with a large enough aquarium so that it can swim freely. It also needs a dry area, where it can rest and sunbathe. For small turtles, you can start with a smaller aquarium, but you should remember that when they are well looked after, turtles can reach a considerable size—10 inches (25 cm) or more—in very little time. Here's a good rule for working out the size of the aquarium: The depth of the water should be between one and a half and two times the length of the shell, with about 8 inches (20 cm) between the surface of the water and the top of the aquarium, so that it can't escape. The width should be between two and three times the length of the shell and the length four to five times that of the shell. For adult turtles, this can mean a very large aquarium. An opaque tank may be used instead of an aquarium, using the dimensions indicated.

The dry part of the aquarium

You must consider that as well as water, the aquarium should have a dry area. There are several solutions: You can place large cemented stones on one side of the tank, piled up until they overhang the tank, also using branches and other decorations to create a flat surface. Another solution consists in sticking a glass surface to one side of the aquarium with a small ramp so that the turtle can get out of the water when it wants to. The surface can be decorated with artificial grass, right up to the water's edge. In specialized shops, you can find aquariums already prepared in this way. The red-eared slider loves the sun. It enjoys sunbathing in its natural environment until reaching a high enough temperature to dive into the water to cool off. It is important to provide your turtle with a daily source of ultraviolet rays, which it needs for its bones and shell to grow healthily and to prevent rickets. Special ultraviolet lamps are available for this purpose. It is also necessary to illuminate the aquarium for eight to twelve hours a day. There are special aquarium lids for attaching the required fluorescent lights.

To complement the aquarium

Before adding the water and rocks, place a thin layer of sand at the bottom of the aquarium. You can also place some decoration in the water, such as a branch, or an upside-down roof tile. The temperature is a very important aspect. These turtles live in hot regions. You should place a water heater in the aquarium, together with a thermometer. The water temperature should be between 75° and 86°F (24° and 30°C). If the temperature is below this range, the turtle may lose its appetite, stop growing, and will be less able to fight off illnesses. It's not good to exceed 86°F (30°C) either. With respect to the dry area, no additional elements are required, as long as the temperature of the room is above 75°F (24°C). You simply need a light bulb to warm the dry area, where the turtle can lie down and warm itself. The temperature of this zone should be about 86–88°F (30–31°C). The turtle should not be able to reach the light bulb under any circumstances. You will also need a water filter, as the Florida turtle feeds in the water and also relieves himself there. The filter should not create too strong a current, as these turtles live in calm water. In any case, the water should always be reasonably clean and even with the filter, it should be changed every three or four weeks, taking advantage of the occasion to clean the bottom of the tank and the rest of the fittings.

More meat when they're small, more greens when they're older

Red-eared sliders are omnivores. This means that they eat foods of both vegetable and animal origin. However, their diet varies according to their age. When they are young, they are mainly carnivorous and must be fed daily. When they are adults, they prefer to eat vegetables, and you can feed them once every two or three days. The diet of both the young and the adults should be varied, so that the turtle can get all the nutrients and vitamins that it needs. Never give them more than they can eat; it's better to be a bit "mean." You can give them ready prepared food for reptiles, available from pet shops, preferably in the form of pellets or solid sticks that don't dirty the water. They can also eat live worms, which you should buy in the shop, because worms from the garden carry many bacteria and parasites. There are other kinds of live food available from specialized shops, such as crickets, small fish, or mosquito larvae. Other sources of animal protein, though they should only be used occasionally, are beef cut into small pieces, cooked chicken, and also fresh cat or dog food. Most of the food you give your turtle should be in the form of vegetables: spinach leaves or fresh cabbage, dandelion, chopped carrot, zucchini, and green beans. They can also eat fresh fruit, such as apples, pears, strawberries, etc., cut into small pieces. They love tomatoes, but you should only give them to turtles very occasionally, like other foodstuffs rich in phosphorous, as they impede the absorption of calcium. Two or three times a week, you should enrich their diet with a little calcium powder mixed with the food. With respect to vitamin supplements, only use them if necessary, as a varied diet and a good source of ultraviolet light provides them with everything they need.

The turtle's health

You should always watch out for possible illnesses that the turtle can contract. If you notice unusual symptoms in the eyes, nostrils, or mouth, if lumps or spots appear on the shell, or if it changes behavior, for example, with a loss of appetite or reduced activity, you should take it to a vet who specializes in reptiles. Nowadays, more and more specialized vets are able to adequately treat turtles. When you bring the turtle home for the first time, it's highly advisable to place it in quarantine for several days. You should prevent it from coming into contact with children during this period. As soon as you are able, you should take a stool sample to the vet for analysis, together with the turtle, for a general checkup. If he or she declares the turtle to be free from danger, that is, with no intestinal parasites or pathogenic bacteria, you can put the turtle in its designated place. With regards to the handling of turtles by children, they must first be old enough to hold the turtle in both hands with no risk of it falling (especially for adult turtles). Second, it is essential to wash your hands before and after picking it up, to prevent infections.

How to choose your turtle

When purchasing a turtle, you should look out for certain features that will help you to select the healthiest turtle. First, the shell should be healthy. Among young turtles, this means a surface that feels like fingernails. With adult turtles, the shell should be hard without any lumps or damaged plates. The skin should also have a healthy appearance without cracks around the neck or legs. The eyes should be open and lively without swelling and should not seem half closed. The nostrils should be clean, without bubbles and emitting no sound. The claws should be strong and complete. Last, the turtle should respond when you pick it up in the air, either by kicking furiously or hiding quickly inside its shell. Both actions are an indication of good health. It doesn't matter if you choose a male or a female (difficult to distinguish when they're very small). It's best to have just one turtle, as this species does not tolerate the presence of a companion very well, except during the mating season. Besides, you would need to add extra space to the aquarium if you wanted to keep two turtles (about 30 percent larger).

English language version published by
Barron's Educational Series, Inc., 2008

Original title of the book in Catalan: *Una tortuga en casa*
© Copyright GEMSER PUBLICATIONS S.L., 2008
Barcelona, Spain
Author: Alejandro Algarra
Translator: Sally-Ann Hopwood
Illustrator: Rosa Maria Curto

All inquiries should be addressed to:
Barron's Educational Series, Inc.
250 Wireless Boulevard
Hauppauge, New York 11788
www.barronseduc.com

ISBN-13: 978-0-7641-4060-0
ISBN-10: 0-7641-4060-4

Library of Congress Catalog Card. No. 2008925894

Printed in China
9 8 7 6 5 4 3 2 1